Thumbprints

Helen Overell

Oversteps Books

First published in 2015 by   Oversteps Books Ltd
                                    6 Halwell House
                                    South Pool
                                    Nr Kingsbridge
                                    Devon
                                    TQ7 2RX
                                    UK

www.overstepsbooks.com

Copyright © 2015 Helen Overell
ISBN 978-1-906856-53-3

All rights reserved. No part of this book may be reproduced, stored in a retrieval system, or transmitted in any form, or by any means, electronic, mechanical, photocopying, recording or otherwise, or translated into any language, without prior written permission from Oversteps Books, except by a reviewer who may quote brief passages in a review.

The right of Helen Overell to be identified as the author of this work has been asserted by her in accordance with the Copyright, Designs and Patents Act 1988.

Printed in Great Britain by imprint digital, Devon

for Paul

Acknowledgements:

A number of these poems or versions of them have appeared in the following magazines: Antiphon, Other Poetry, Qarrtsiluni, Scintilla and The Interpreter's House.

Some of these poems were shortlisted or commended in the following competitions: Bedford Open Poetry Competition 2012, Cinnamon Press Single Poem Competition 2013, The Frogmore Prize 2014, the Troubadour Open Poetry Competition 2012 and the Poetry Society Stanza Competition 2014.

Contents

Kaleidoscope	1
Cobweb	2
Astrocytoma	3
Cello Suite No. 5 in C minor, J S Bach	4
Effigy	5
Magpie	6
One for sorrow	6
Two for joy	7
In folklore	8
St Joseph's	9
Cora	9
Annie	10
Sarah	11
Hettie	12
Day room	13
Margaret	14
Rosie	15
Mary	16
One small step	17
Salisbury	18
Maths	19
Warsaw Ghetto	20
From behind her	21
Outreach	22
The Abigail	23
Late of this dwelling place	24
The Mercedes	25
Pebble	26
Another Place	27
Mexican votive paintings	28
Jordan	29
National Archaeological Museum, Amman	29
Goats	30
Mount Nebo	31
Petra	32
Sunset	33

Lacemakers, Chartres	34
Leeks	35
Tea at Polesden Lacey	36
Shelter	37
Observing the boundary from within	38
Cave painting — South Africa	39
Cloud mountain	40
Parrog	41
Harmony	42
Quadrat	43
New Malden	44
Letting go	45
Gone	46
Emergence	47
Embankment	47
Charing Cross	47
Waterloo	47
Along the Waterloo line	48
Artefact	49
Cui Hen Beudy	50
Amulet	51

Kaleidoscope

The closed and cuffed cardboard tube whispers
when shaken, and when held towards the light

marvels burst into being — pink and gold, blue
and green — petals as bright as buttercups or

spurred and even geometries of snow or else
a single straight-edged cell fit for a honeycomb,

each giving way with jostled sigh at the least
shift of wrist, the exact slip that filters light

never the same again; and with steady hand,
this can be passed to you — the vision shared.

Cobweb

Hawthorn, rose-hip, weathered fern
and, mid-air, lace as intricate

as any worked from flax, as fine,
and every strand a deep curve

strung with beads, worlds full of sky,
up-turned trees, a skim of ground;

and our breath lost in the mist,
and all held in globes of light.

Astrocytoma
for FG

The moon's in hiding,
pared to the rim of a fine
porcelain bowl,

the far edge
cloaked by a swirling
skim of steam.

The girl, pale
as dregs of day, her face
round as the clock

on the wall that inches
time, grasps the deep
flat-based spoon

in the hand that obeys
thought, scoops, leans in, sips
the comfort of mushrooms.

Her throat, in training,
swallows, warmth trickles
through her bones.

She is enfolded
in the quiet of stars,
has returned again

from the onslaught
that seeks to oust the dark
clutch of overgrowth

lodged within her head
that undoes her walking, puts
her days on hold.

Cello Suite No. 5 in C minor, J S Bach

This half-hour alone with you, with Bach,
the well-made coffin, the wreath
laid bright above your silence — deeper
now than those you used to keep;

age had unravelled you, diminished
your dreams, withered muscle, bone, tendon,
seeped into your lungs — each breath burned, chewed
small sad holes inside your head;

music fills the room — long sombre notes
weave sound to solemn fugue; the 'cello
mourns — resonant, bereft; the burden
begins to ease

Effigy

Skin-skimmed bone —
an involution of close-folded
wings above stepped ribs
arching from a backbone
made of threaded pebbles;
pelvis white as flint,
face to the wall,
knees drawn up,
the world shut out.

Yet when he calls her name,
stone is undone, she turns
her head towards him, eyes
deep shivered wells
fractured with light.

Magpie

I

One for sorrow

Gutspill on the winding road
that leads to Ranmore —

flattened pelt of rabbit
on the tarmac —

a solitary magpie already on patrol,
hopping sideways on both legs;

my sister in Suffolk would salute him
with *Hello Sir*,

my Polish friend blows kisses,
remembers how she saw

three magpies just before her first labour,
how the baby was a girl;

so now I play safe — my greeting
sotto voce, my lips pursed,

after all, this bird has clout,
stands alone —

legend tells of his refusal to enter
Noah's Ark — has him

sitting on the roof and swearing
for the duration.

II

Two for joy

Both are perched on the branch of a hawthorn tree,
squinting into the long low light of morning.

He sees a field full of diamonds, he swoops down,
eyes the encrusted blades of grass,

pecks at fire, his thirst remains unquenched,
he is disheartened, disconsolate.

She tugs on a glint of silver, frees a thread fine
as angel hair, a tatter of last year's tinsel,

foil to the berries, dark as blood, the ragged leaves
in wearied green, the needles of shadow-spikes.

She flies to the nest — the ravelling trails
from her beak — tethers, tucks the strand

amongst bits of wire, sticks that make the dome
that shelters them, until a steady radiance,

as from a single star, lightens his heart, hers,
makes clear the sky, the path beneath.

III

In folklore

when all the birds of the world
sang to comfort

the One on the cross dying, the pied
chatterer made no sound

but then he must have known
his call to be hoarse —

rusty iron rasping on sore-throated
stone — he must have sensed

song to be other, spared the sorrowing
chorus, beak tight shut.

St Joseph's

I

Cora

Cora's ears are large — seem too big for her head,
her face is a humour of creases, a lit paper lantern,
her fine slate-dark hair, cut all one length, tucks
into the nape of her neck, brushes her chin,

she is frail, slight as a child, her skin stretched
taut over delicate bones, ink-blue veins, the steady
pulse that beats at her neck; her hands — knuckle
heavy — rest on the counterpane,

Sister Dominic — all cushioned gray, sleeves rolled
to elbow, veil wayward as a blackbird in a dustbath —
turns to me *Cora used to be a teacher* she says,
isn't that right now? she adds,

leaning in towards the pillows, Cora smiles, eyes
pools of light, the whisper-loud answer can barely
be heard, Sister smooths Cora's forehead, *Her son
visits every week-end* she tells me,

isn't that so? she adds nodding to Cora, tidying
bedclothes to comfort. Cora eases into memories,
her thoughts fold inwards; we walk on, our feet
squeak on the polished linoleum.

II

Annie

Back to the wall, Annie tenses for sound,
sits on the edge of her chair — all round the room,
old people doze, blink awake, nod off;

the end of my shift is in sight, afternoon light
pours through the out-of-reach windows, pools
on the swirls of a rough square of carpet;

Annie hears my footsteps, grasps my greeting, clings
to my hands, my arms, *Don't leave me here all alone
in the dark* she says over and over,

undoing the calm; the nun in the doorway — veiled,
steel gray, forehead half-hidden by oblonged white —
looks at the clock, tuts, tells me to go;

wrist over fist, my smooth freckled skin slips free
from the grip of slithered knots in roped veins;
the cries tangle, stay trapped in my head.

III

Sarah

They said she had fallen —
though there were no marks
on her — they took him away,
she knew then without doubt
her heart was past mending.

They brought her to a place
out of town, handed her over,
never came back. She was taken
in here — fit, strong, willing —
when the asylum closed.

Sarah spoons tiny morsels
into Hettie's bird-gape mouth,
pours coffee, sees that Annie
sips the sweetened milky drink,
her work-shift never stops.

IV

Hettie

Jabbed elbows, restless wrists, Hettie perches
on an upright chair, spends all day at the loom,
winds bobbins, tugs threads, weaves cloth, her hair
fluffed white, her blue eyes faded, her head nods,
her stubbed tongue works at words no-one can hear.

Sarah tidies her Courtelle jumper, Bri-Nylon slacks,
puts back her slippered heels, her face beams;
her clog-heavy feet are wadded with cotton waste,
the roar of the mill drowns out her own heart-beat,
mouths the bone-shudder ache that stalks every shift.

V

Day room

Windows out of reach, doors double-locked,
an arrangement of armchairs on a swirled carpet,

stockings anchored with looped and bobbled
knots just below the knee, thumbed into comfort,

Crimplene dresses, Bri-Nylon slacks, knitted cardigans,
heads nod, eyes close on dreams, the morning drifts;

rattle of keys, the lunchtime trolley — all mirrored
shine, puffs of steam, hint of cabbage and custard,

the slow shuffled rise to sit at the table, Rosie
shepherded, Margaret led by the hand, blind Annie

coaxed and comforted, restless Hettie soothed
and settled, mince and mashed potato spooned out

onto plates — the bluff good humour of stalwart
Sarah without whom we would indeed be lost.

VI

Margaret

After the meal, the clearing of table to trolley,
the double unlocking and locking of doors,
the securing of keys,

the steady shuffle from day room to toilet, an arm
offered here, a walking stick held ready there,
feet settled into slippers,

Margaret is lost, the slow slide into childhood
has turned knee-length knickers
to an elasticated nightmare —

Sarah chivvies her on, waits with her, tidies her up,
soothes her whimpers, talks of the day
when her health and strength

will surely return, though Margaret has slipped
through the gap, stands the other side of speech,
has lost all meaning.

VII

Rosie

Rosie, deep in her armchair,
dozes the whole morning through,
head tilted, chin propped on folded
hands, her face creased,

her dress, in rumpled folds,
blue as the chipped painted gown
on the *Our Lady* statue stood
on a shelf out of harm's way.

Rosie wakes up for lunch,
eats every last morsel, wanders off
down the corridor to the parlour
where imprints of visitors

balance dutiful tea-cups
on bone-thin saucers, nibble dry
wafer biscuits. No-one is there.
Sarah finds her searching

behind chairs, curtains, tables.
What are you looking for, Rosie? she asks,
taking her hand. *Angels*, Rosie says,
her face is bright.

VIII

Mary

No taller than a child, she scurries
from kitchen to pantry, laundry to drying room.

She has no words, reads lips, eyes, faces, takes meaning
from gestures, her smile fills the basement corridors.

The tumour saps her strength, her eyes are dark with pain,
she turns food away, curls up under her bedclothes.

For days, the sisters take turns, moisten her dry mouth,
stroke her hands, keep watch beside her, pray for her soul.

One small step

The encumbered, four-limbed ghosts — bulked joints
awkward as nested tyres — captured on film.

In one full-body snap, the visored face
holds the cameraman — proof of presence.

His feet are planted on the stone-still sea;
he has disturbed the sifted shallows.

From his heels, trail straggled shadows, ribbon
flat — an alien species, black as void.

There is nothing to refract the light —
the image is clear, sharp, unwavering.

Both are drenched in star-blaze that bounces
back, forth, bold as meteor-strike.

All they have known — the blue swirl of earth —
floats in the sky, can be cupped in one hand.

And now there are footprints on the moon,
the tread of boots forever in the dust.

Salisbury
Walking Madonna by Elizabeth Frink

The winter cygnet eyes us, feathers dun, sand,
the gray that rivers take to heart when sky
slips out of thin blue homespun,
puts on dusk.

Willows guard the bank, bear calloused
scars on coppiced crowns, withstand the bluff
chill-fingered wind — we look up,
sculpted saints

throng the cathedral wall, we see the great spire
tilt, bear down from the racing sky, torn clouds catch
on outcrops of worn stone, haul the dizzy weight back,
we are spared.

We walk away, draw near to the woman — forehead
scarved in the way of wimples — who strides out
unhampered by her long robes, bronzed,
features gaunt,

sure of the way, of her work, at home in her soul,
her child within the world, the tug of her heart,
her open hands big with gentling light, blessed
by his touch.

Maths

How these girls love to learn —
scarved heads bent over books,

numbers in rows, columns,
pencilled lines, neat courage

underlined in blueblack
ink — each drop guarded, eked

out — all of them adept
now in the market place;

the next step, forbidden
territory, calls on

diligence, abstract thought,
deducing the unknown —

algebra — we teach this
at our peril, the death

threats hiss in my pocket,
fisted to crumpled flame;

my flock of swallows waits,
we begin as always

with what we think we know —
apricots, figs, assign

symbols, equate harvest
with rainfall, solve simple

partnerships, chalk on board,
damp rag around my hand;

no notes, only the swoop
as thought soars when the link

takes hold, the spark ignites,
another world unfolds

as though pistachios
opened up to show sky

ablaze with mapped out stars
too numerous to count.

Warsaw Ghetto

i.m. Irena Sendlerowa 15 Feb 1910 — 12 May 2008

Cigarette papers   thin, flimsy,
                                      easily hidden

and on each one   written small, neat
                                      in the same hand

there are two names   the given, birth name —
                                         Old Testament patronymic

                                         the chosen substitute —
                                         formal foster-link

these are packed tight   into two glass jars
                                         with screw-top lids,

                                         buried in the garden
                                         against the day

                                         the world's madness
                                         will surely end

each paper a passport   for a child given over,
                                         smuggled out in a tool box

                                         for a child given over,
                                         hurried through the sewers

                                         for a child given over —
                                         stitched yellow star left behind.

Irena Sendlerowa was a Polish Catholic social worker who served in the Polish Underground and the Zegota resistance organization in German-occupied Warsaw during World War II.

From behind her
for Dita

Towards the end — stubbled eggshell skull, skin
cleaved to bone — on the forced march beyond the barbed wire,
her knees buckle, women either side prop her up,

all are herded into a barn, the great doors closed,
thirst cracks her lips, kindles fire in her fissured throat,
fallen ghosts keen in her sleep;

day breaks with no sound — the yard a blank stare,
faded stars in the sweep of morning;

the allies, haunted now and always, greet
wraiths with dulled eyes, wisped breath,
share out rations, do what they can;

and then the lone journey back to her country,
her village, surely her father will make his way home,
every train draws her, holds her;

another emptied platform, her hands fall by her sides,
behind her, he half-sobs her name.

Outreach

One old penny
took me one step
further up the ladder,

my name written
small on each rung,
and, at the top,

the reward —
to choose a saint's name
for a child in Africa

and so an infant
became a namesake
for a saint overseas,

and, in the mission
school, was taught
right from wrong.

Years on, all of us grown,
so many miracles
in doubt,

there must be those
whose name bestowed
without question

no longer fits,
those whose mismatch
never did.

The Abigail

The girl weeps, raw-knuckled, mops
the laundered tide of spindrift suds —
no more thimbled hems, billowed oceans
anchored on an aproned lap,

sheets turned sides-to-middle, clothes pinned
and tucked and put to rights, tiny stitches
battening the warp and weft of cloth,
darning fine as damassin,

no need now for a lass to help mend linen,
fingers nimble, eyes young enough to see
the ply of needle, to thread the eye
with cotton twist,

The Abigail replaces her, dark as night,
the name in lettered gold within the hooped frame,
the round black flat-bed, the hand-turned wheel,
all inlaid with tiny flakes,

white & pink & green, that catch the light,
lustrous as tumbled shells, the whole steady
as gimbals in a squall at sea; the murmured whirr
drowns out confidences

tucked inside the folds of hand-stitched seams
layered with lavender; the thread unspools to looped
links in a neat line as though a skilled seamstress
labours unseen.

Late of this dwelling place
i.m. Sheila

She would have delighted
in the oblong of noon-sky silk,
the obi in leaf-green,
the translucent paper nest.

She would have unfolded
the kimono, watched
cornered sleeves flow
from one to another.

She would have raised
the neckline to her own,
felt the weight of threads
petalled pink on gold.

She would have marvelled
at the chrysanthemums —
those tiny even stitches,
that painstaking detail.

She would have held
the garment at arm's length,
seen the cherry blossom —
the fleetingness of life.

She would have looked
into his eyes, no words
needed, his arms alongside
hers, the robe around her,

and she would have been
transformed, her gingham
apron out of sight, his gift
himself, safe home.

The Mercedes
for VS

already old as the African hills
when given to her father
as part of his annual pay
in the days he worked at the paper mill —

each journey a slow,
stately, considered trek —
and when he passed on,
handed over to a farmer who was known

to be gifted in all
the ways and inner
workings of engines, outer
matters of tyres and chipped paint, called

into new life, driven
the while, as well-befitted,
with dignity and decorum,
by the Zulu driver, now an aged man

who, she is told, retired
well into his eighties, his gift
the key — overcome, he sank
to the ground, *I have no power* he said.

And the great machine
dwells in his village,
polished, every Saturday,
without fail, to a dazzle of a gleam;

she hears how the whole
family, dressed in Sunday
best, is carried to Church, then
on to the Spar for the weekly shop, the low

hum of the laden car
content as any burdened
in the long lull of a life,
the deep bass notes a wordless Hallelujah.

Pebble

Lodged in a stretch of sand,
tugged seaward by the slow
silk flow of salt water,
sky torn by cries of gulls,
the single small stone,
bleached white as bone,
bears a thrift-pink fern
cast adrift from the deep
as though drawn with pen
and indelible ink —
bold as tumbled waves
on a rock-pool shore,
clear as trailed lace
on marl, basalt, slate.

Another Place
from Another Place by Antony Gormley

He stands ankle-deep in shingle, looking ahead
towards offshore sky, he is buffeted by the wind.

The tide turns, waves roll in gritty with sand,
rust-red ribbons of seaweed cling, slip aside.

He is up to his knees in the rain-pitted swell,
pays no heed, ignores the quarrels of gulls.

He is wreathed in sea-fret, he wears manacles
made from wisps of mist, he is covered in barnacles.

He shoulders the ocean, tugged by the undertow,
nibbled by quicksilver fish in dizzy shoals.

His face is crusted with salt, he keeps
his gaze on the smudged horizon, does not sleep.

The ebb leaves him stranded, brothers out of reach,
a gathering of distances, guardians on watch.

Mexican votive paintings

The lost child
found,

the missing herd of goats
retrieved,

accidents with ladders, lorries,
survived,

tumours, as big as an avocado,
shrunk;

the stories in bold brush-strokes
on roof tiles

made of tin, fastened inside a church,
lit by candles;

on most, emblazoned above the stricken
son, daughter —

the Lady; on some the burdened cross
or else the saint;

the vigil in faith,
vivid;

here a line, *Doy Gracias a San
Francisco de Asis*

*por haberme salvado de este
accidente,*

unsigned, the artist
paid

in small coins —
enough for bread.

Jordan

I

National Archaeological Museum, Amman

No explanations allowed in the museum —
printed in bold beneath a counterflow of curves.

A small child sleeps, tucked up in sand, shielded by glass,
forever crouched, skull too big for fine laddered ribs.

Burial pots in lidded earthenware complete
with moulded faces, formal arms, lean upright

against a wall, empty now, the three full-grown
skeletons that stood in each, nowhere to be seen.

Flasks for tears, blown glass, with narrow fluted necks, gathered
in a motley group, sigh, hold only salt sorrow.

We meander into the bright heat, the air loud
with calls to evening prayer — spindled minarets inked

on the sky, brushed by sifts of light that dust sparrows
in the olive trees, skim flat roofs in falcon flight.

II

Goats

The minibus groans, grinds into gear,
the view swings full circle;

dry scree skitters as the throttle roars,
we judder to a halt,

the brash brown road blocked, the brake-slip slope
occupied by locals;

we see a solid heap of pieced fur —
sienna, chocolate, cream —

a huddle of goats, their folded flanks
tucked against bony rumps,

their doze — chin by flopped ear; the herdsman
shouts, waves his arms; they rise,

ragged, startled, on slow, stick-thin legs,
drowse-heavy — the neat quilt

unpicked, the counterpane
undone — scatter to scant

scrub, sparse growth beside the olive trees
dusted to silver-gray,

wild irises, the bright red poppy
pickings at the road's edge;

nimble-footed, ruminant, they stare,
embedded in the land;

sheer willpower starts the bus again,
removes us from their gaze.

III

Mount Nebo

The sifted light
falls at our feet,
we tread on dust, dry rock,
scattered shadows —
        fans with splayed ribs
        fine as darning needles —
we breathe sunbeaten air,
cool resin draughts;

the path rises,
hugs the rounded mountain shoulder,
we look out on the wing steep fall,
as Moses did —
        the promised land,
        mapped in arrows engraved in bronze;

beside us, in spun steel, tree-tall,
staff and serpent intertwined,
etch an outlined cross
onto the baked sky,
        blessing all regardless,

while small birds flit,
stitch nests where nails
would once have been,
        sing psalms threaded
        with glad salaams,

as though chirp loud flocks
depicted in the hunkered church
behind us —
        in pieced clay, chipped stone,

had flown from underfoot.

IV

Petra

The child shadows me, shows me
stones he has found here — skewed
gray cubes with white bands,
rose-red flakes —

he wants me to buy them, sighs
at my reluctance, *Business not good
today* — such troubled words
for one not yet six;

the first boy sold me postcards,
fingered the logo on my purse —
three lime yellow planes glide
on a night sky —

he watched me mime *Flight*,
grinned, purred an engine roar —
swooped and wheeled, his arms
outstretched wings;

my sister opens up a family-size
packet of crisps, gives these out
in handfuls, includes the urchins
who stand close by,

lean against the rocks in the scant
mid-morning shade, taking a break —
the young stone merchant lolls,
salt thumb on tongue.

V

Sunset

Heat pours in solid waves
through the unshuttered window,

dry gusts of wind pummel
the walls with angry sighs,

trickle desert sand
over faded floors,

swirl dust into whorls
distinct as finger prints.

Beyond the window,
olive trees flicker

silver lightnings
across unshielded sky,

tug at the stars, ease
constellations into sight.

Lacemakers, Chartres

Cloaked in black, seated on *prie-dieux*
outside the cathedral walls,

bonnets nod over pillows of straw
patterned with knuckle-tall pins,

fine linen thread looped into braids
anchored with bobbins of bone;

gnarled winter hands coax intricate knots
into buds, leaves, flowers —

murmured novenas woven to endure —
swirls rimmed with frost lifted whole

from a window pane on a plummet cold
night encrusted with stars.

Leeks

The leeks are at the hairpin stage,
later, they will straighten:

leek seedlings, days old
and still in polystyrene pods

droop as though all hope is lost,
bend at the waist in semaphore,

signal distress; mystified, I peer
at the wisps, fine as grass,

the small hoops — vivid green —
only just emerged, at the taller,

feet-firm stage, almost ready
to let go, stand hands-free

and finger-tipped with spent
brown seed case —

an angled reach, a slow raise
from stoop to almost

upright and those fast gaining
height — and I wonder

how, in all these years,
this has escaped me,

slow growth in steady stages,
each with a wisdom

that guides and encourages
the unfolded self —

leaves behind what is outgrown,
moves towards light.

Tea at Polesden Lacey
for ML

We sit at a table near the window,
all talk and lilted laughter, stills of thought.

A small girl, carrying a blue bag, walks
towards us through the forest of chair legs,

halts, looks me in the eye, says nothing but
something in her stance is an unsung song —

What do you have there? I ask, she shows me
the folded oblong of silver paper

carried with such care within the sky depths,
that is all there is, *Oh* I say, polite

and kind, whereupon she reaches inside,
fetches out, in pincer grip, a nothing,

places this on my outstretched palm then turns
to go, my thanks acknowledged with a nod.

Can I have one? asks my friend and, with due
diligence, another is found, given.

The child wanders off to where her mother
sips tea, chats, keeps watch. We sit with our gifts,

not knowing quite what to do — the tiny
objects without substance rest in our hands.

Our dilemma is noticed, our donor
marches back to us, takes a deep breath and

squares her shoulders, *Put it in your pocket,*
she tells us *it's a penny* she explains.

And so this we do, stowing away coins
we cannot see or feel against hard times.

Shelter

At first it was only a game —
dragged from sleep by the sirens' wail,
rushed under the stairs by her mother,
squeezed in with her brothers, and one
dared to draw on the wall —
soldiers with bayonets.

It went on, so men dug a pit
at the garden's end, put a roof in place,
piled all the earth on top, there were beds
in the Anderson shelter, slick
smells of damp concrete, mud —
water oozed in, sleep fled.

No end in sight — the Morrison
fitted indoors, made of metal, a sturdy
over-sized table with draw-down mesh
walls against shrapnel *Only Hitler
throwing his pots downstairs*
her father would say,

his arms around them and
that saw them through; after, the grassed
mound outside — mountain, castle-keep,
ship's crows-nest — her look-out, hands
as telescope, all along the back
gardens whose boundary,

the embankment, had saved them,
lifted the snarl-silenced doodlebug over
the tracks to make ghosts on the other
side — the thud worse than thunder,
sudden trains in the night,
her heart pounding, after.

Observing the boundary from within

Midsummer and the sheer green of outlook —
exuberance of leaf on shrub —

pebbled shallows in the window-glaze discard
detail for an abstract flood,

north-cold, and this casts blue-grey shadows
on the work-top, dampens

the oriental reds and golds of the slippered
figures on the tea caddy;

at nightfall, the dark expanse is interrupted
by a ragged patch of light

that spills from our neighbour's house, dances
in a broken glow as though

hand-held at shoulder-height, a lantern to guide
the stranger far from home.

Cave painting — South Africa

In the flicker of firelight,
solid rock sways,

yet here in the shadow-deep
dark of the cave

only the eland can make way
between this world

and the other — no man or
young-bearer, child,

lion, leopard or great snake
can slip through

this curtain-wall of cold stone,
this threshold-skim;

so here we see just the painted
curves of back and

neck and head — the flank and legs
remain

still in the spirit home,
the sensed unseen.

Cloud mountain

Rain solid as a falling river
blurs the chapel barn to
rippled rock —

a blackbird perches on the roof —
wings at half-mast,
beak to the sky —

rinsed and pounded —
feathers cleansed,
thirst appeased,

the steep, green-gold
rise of bracken draped
in a sky-shroud.

Parrog

We walk on sky that is mirrored in sand,
waves purl, ebb, steal our footprints.

We talk about gravity, curved space-time,
how moments on Earth are greater

than those in orbit, as Einstein predicted
from the twenty-six Maxwell

equations funnelled into just four —
an understated quartet.

We sit on clumps of marram planted
to keep the land in check.

We watch as the sea undoes the horizon,
merges with layers of dull cloud,

shrinks distances to gradations of gray
that sift and shift, although black

rocks remain, as do hardy walkers in red
cagoules, dogs chasing the tide.

There is a shiver, the faintest shadow,
and we look up, startled, far

above the *parrog*, a shift in the firmament,
a rift rimmed with molten stars

burns with fierce light, an outspill of silver
floods the strand.

Parrog: Welsh: harbour

Harmony
Pembrokeshire

We see two men seated mid-slope
on a blue tarpaulined roof,

we travel closer, another crouches
on scaffolding at run-off height —

the gutter clings, tenacious, the rain
could slide in sheets at any moment —

one more pours from a Thermos flask,
mugs are handed round as though

all four were perched on boulders
on a hillside, ankle-deep in heather,

instead of being half-way to heaven,
within sight of the ever-present sea;

we drive on past the gable end
where the name — *Harmony Chapel* —

stands out above the tall double
doors for all to see; beyond, tomb-

stones — inscribed slate, chiselled stone — tilt
together in good-natured rows,

then a handful of houses, nothing more;
the sky like a sail billowing in the wind,

held fast by the ridge of the blue
tarpaulined roof, sheltering the men,

those indoors, the children playing
hide-and-seek, the bones asleep.

Quadrat

An infinity of sky, and the moor an ocean of heather,
and in the space framed by the low throw of a quadrat —

the tread of a path, sphagnum moss, tufted sheep's tail grass,
yellow tormentil, rust-red sundew, ghost-green lichen —

a tapestry so detailed, each stitch, observed through a hand lens,
opens the way into the needle's eye, the world within.

New Malden

Suburban semis doze
in the mid-morning hush
that laps the railway lines,
floods fishbone avenues;

the horse-chestnut — branches
bare, trunk multi-pollarded —
stands at the kerb, watches
with a thousand eyes;

camellias — tethered and
fenced — white violets in
an unmown lawn, join
the magnolia in prayer;

and a sudden blackbird
sings a psalm unseen.

Letting go

The silver birch is clothed in gold, in shimmered
fountain-fall, as though each leaf were a bead

strung onto threads eased from weft of sky
and these beaded lengths fastened as a fringe

to a shawl that dips and sways about the tree —
all grace and warmth and gathered light —

and this holds fast until, one after another —
whispered entreaty, thumbed and mouthed

cadences of sound both familiar and strange,
moments filled with still and pooled silences —

the leaves loosen, let go, drift and float,
bright whirls in flung and fluttered flame.

Gone

The choke of it
and blackthorn white with grief,

the shock
and senses numb, the swan

upon the water
still as tears that will not flow,

the mind's core
frozen and yet the tasks

done — the table
set, fresh tea in the pot —

the world
imploded, heavy in my hand,

your thumbprint
on the lifeline in my palm.

Emergence

Embankment

Morning coffee
in a cardboard cup, mown grass,
a bandstand — past echoes of trumpets,
euphoniums, trombones, rousing speeches —
dossers doze in deckchairs; he walks
to a bench, sits, thinks, beside
the slow September
Thames.

Charing Cross

A poem,
by a Polish poet,
written out in English,
pasted on the tunnel wall,
stops her mid-stride,
taps at her heart.

Waterloo

Bruised sky,
long shadows of evening,
great chunks of double rainbow
braced mid-air between one tall building
and the next — an iridescent
glory to lighten steps,
his, hers — hands,
breath held.

Along the Waterloo line

Another graveyard —
staggered tombstones,
rattled bones,

railings keep
bewildered ghosts
from trespass,

bindweed haunts
flimsy outlines:
top-hatted

strollers, dreamers,
chasers of hoops —
fleet of foot,

swaddled infants,
all ailments gone;

we are blurs

in boxes, cooped up,
rolled on metal rails,
we flicker

past, faint shadows
from the future,
out of sight.

Artefact

An ancient flat stone
        chiselled into life —

two men plough a field,
        using two yoked cows —

one man walks behind,
        he wields a long stick,

the other, in front,
        holds a branch with leaves.

Scholars muse for hours —
        The stick strikes the cows,

drives the beasts that drag
        the plough that makes drills

in the field; the branch
        with leaves? who can say?

Then in Spain one day
        a learned scholar

sees two old men plough
        using two yoked cows,

one long stick, one branch
        with leaves — the first man

waves the branch to keep
        flies away, to swish

leaf cool air around
        the working beasts' eyes,

the other pauses
        at each furrow's end

scrapes the plough blade clean
        with his long stout stick.

Cui Hen Beudy

Petals, no bigger than apostrophes, rain
down on us, lay scattered at our feet —
bright perforations in the solid earth,
lit as though by star-fire deep beneath;

hawthorn blossom is now a drift of light —
branches on the may tree are green again,
each twig beaded, in every shade of ragged
leaf, with clustered haws in slow formation;

the chapel barn looks out on mountains,
river valley, sky — we linger at the gate,
safe as in the storm porch of a weathered
church, our vows renewed, keeping faith.

Amulet

The points on the clipped paper disc
wrap round the rim of a small coin

and in ink, in an even hand,
on the very edge, the *Lord's Prayer*

begins, curves into a spiral
and after *Amen*, George Yeofound

wrote his name, age — 88 years —
and the place and date — Southampton,

9th September, eighteen hundred
and seventy two — the text leaps

under the magnifying lens
in the display case *hallowed be*

thy name and *our daily bread* and
forgive us weighted with *as we*

forgive and then *deliver us
from evil* and this was carried

by a soldier in the Great War —
and the words resound as loud now

as murmured when written so clear
within the space of a thumbprint.

This amulet is in the collection amassed by Edward Lovett 1852–1933 and displayed in the exhibition The Solace of Objects at the Wellcome Collection.

Oversteps Books Ltd

The Oversteps list includes books by the following poets:

David Grubb, Giles Goodland, Alex Smith, Will Daunt, Patricia Bishop, Christopher Cook, Jan Farquarson, Charles Hadfield, Mandy Pannett, Doris Hulme, James Cole, Helen Kitson, Bill Headdon, Avril Bruton, Marianne Larsen, Anne Lewis-Smith, Mary Maher, Genista Lewes, Miriam Darlington, Anne Born, Glen Phillips, Rebecca Gethin, W H Petty, Melanie Penycate, Andrew Nightingale, Caroline Carver, John Stuart, Rose Cook, Jenny Hope, Hilary Elfick, Jennie Osborne, Anne Stewart, Oz Hardwick, Angela Stoner, Terry Gifford, Michael Swan, Denise Bennett, Maggie Butt, Anthony Watts, Joan McGavin, Robert Stein, Graham High, Ross Cogan, Ann Kelley, A C Clarke, Diane Tang, Susan Taylor, R V Bailey, John Daniel, Alwyn Marriage, Simon Williams, Kathleen Kummer, Jean Atkin, Charles Bennett, Elisabeth Rowe, Marie Marshall, Ken Head, Robert Cole, Cora Greenhill, John Torrance, Michael Bayley, Christopher North, Simon Richey, Lynn Roberts, Sue Davies, Mark Totterdell, Michael Thomas and Ann Segrave.

For details of all these books, information about Oversteps and up-to-date news, please look at our website and blog:

www.overstepsbooks.com
http://overstepsbooks.wordpress.com